AF374090

ORIGINAL

by

DESIGN

A brand so authentic, it sells itself

Jaclynn Buchanan

For Lee, who married a dreamer and never once asked her to dream smaller.

You believed in every single idea.

You partnered with me in every season and always made space for where God was taking us. I would not be here without you.

Now.

Contents

A Note from Me to You

Before we dive in, I want to tell you a little about who I am. Because I think it matters.

My name is Jaclynn Buchanan. I am a creator, an entrepreneur, and someone who has spent a significant part of her life building things that started as nothing more than a feeling in her chest. A nudge. A pull. A quiet voice saying: this is for you.

I believe that voice comes from God.

I have always been a people person. Not in the surface-level, make-small-talk-at-parties kind of way. I mean the kind of person who genuinely lights up when she sees something in someone that they cannot yet see in themselves. From the time I was a little girl, people told me I was a good friend. And looking back, I think what they were really saying was that I paid attention. I saw potential in people before they saw it in themselves, and something in me always wanted to draw that out.

I never chased popularity. Fitting into a mold to be liked by everyone was never my goal. I just wanted to be myself and love people well. I was drawn to the person in the room who had something incredible in them that the world had not discovered yet. That part of me has never changed.

*My goal was never to be liked by everyone.
It was to see the gold in people and help
them see it too.*

I also had a creative, entrepreneurial spirit from as far back as I can remember. I was the kid putting on shows in the backyard, making movies, selling tickets to neighborhood obstacle courses, and yes, making bubble gum and snow cones to sell to anyone who would buy them. If I could dream it up, I was figuring out how to make it real. That instinct never went away. It just grew with me.

As I got older, I found my way into the fashion industry, and that world became one of my greatest classrooms. I learned very quickly that my driving force was not to be the one who received all the accolades. What truly fulfilled me was supporting others and bringing out the best in their dreams. Elevating what someone else was building, making it bigger than life, more intentional, more extraordinary than what anyone expected, and watching them shine in it. That was the thing that lit me up. And I did it well. I poured everything into it and I loved every moment.

What that season gave me, more than any title or credit, was a deep understanding of how to remain completely, unapologetically yourself and still build something great. How to bring your full voice, your full vision, your full self into the work without shrinking it to fit someone else's idea of what belongs there. That knowledge is the foundation of everything in this book.

I believe God wires us from the beginning with everything we need for what we are called to do. Looking back, I can see that the little girl selling snow cones, the loyal friend who always saw the gold in people, and the woman who found her greatest joy in elevating others were all the same person moving toward the same calling. Nothing was wasted.

That calling eventually led me to found Good Day Agency, born out of a deep conviction that creators in the entertainment industry deserved someone in their corner who would protect their authenticity and call them higher. Before that, there was Jaclynn Belts, a creative project built entirely out of passion that taught me everything I now teach others. We will get to that story.

God is woven into my story and into this book. Not as a decoration or a disclaimer, but as the foundation. Every gift, every talent, every passion you carry was placed in you intentionally by a God who knew you before you knew yourself. This book is simply about helping you uncover what He already put there and trust yourself enough to let it shine. That is what we are here to do.

So let us make a deal: I will be fully honest with you, and you give yourself permission to be fully honest with yourself. That is where everything begins.

Let's go.

Introduction

The Magic of Being Unapologetically You

Imagine waking up each morning knowing that everything you do, the way you show up, the way you create, the way you earn a living, is an expression of your true self.

No pretending. No exhausting attempts to fit into someone else's mold. No shrinking yourself down to make other people comfortable. Just you, in all your brilliance, making an impact simply by being exactly who you were always meant to be.

That is the power of a personal brand rooted in authenticity. And I am here to tell you that it is not only possible. It is something you were designed for. God did not place gifts in you so they could stay hidden.

What truly captures attention isn't perfection. It's realness.

We live in an age where the digital world is saturated with polished, picture-perfect personas. Social media is flooded with highlight reels, carefully curated aesthetics, and strategic brand messaging. But here is the secret most people overlook: people are tired of perfect. They are hungry for real.

They do not want another airbrushed, algorithm-optimized personality. They want you. They want to connect with someone who is not afraid to be seen. Someone whose story, struggles, and passions make them feel a little less alone in the world.

Think about the people who have made the deepest impact on you. Not the ones with the best production quality. The ones who made you feel something. The ones who were brave enough to show up exactly as they were.

God does not make mistakes. The specific combination of gifts, experiences, quirks, and passions He placed in you was entirely intentional. Your brand is not something you have to manufacture. It is something He already gave you. Your job is to steward it well.

By the time you finish this book, you will have a clear roadmap for discovering your natural talents, crafting a brand that is unmistakably yours, and turning that authenticity into a sustainable, joyful, and profitable life.

This is not about becoming Instagram famous. This is about building something real, something that creates meaning for you and impact for others.

I want you to think about this book less like a manual and more like a mirror. Every chapter is designed to reflect something back to you, something you may already know but have not yet given yourself permission to act on. The principles are simple. The work of actually living them is where most people get stuck. My job is to walk with you through that.

I have been in rooms with people who had everything the world said you need to succeed and still felt like something was missing. And I have been in rooms with people who had nothing on paper but an unwavering sense of who they were and what they were called to do, and I watched those people build something extraordinary. The difference was never talent. It was always clarity. Clarity about who they were, what they stood for, and why it mattered. That clarity is what we are building here.

I have spent years in the business of helping people build brands and creative careers, and the single most consistent thing I have observed is this: the people who build something lasting are not necessarily the most talented or the most strategic. They are the ones who are the most honest. Honest about who they are, what they care about, and who they are trying to serve. Honesty has a frequency to it that people can feel across a screen. You cannot fake it and you cannot manufacture it. But you can cultivate it, by doing the work this book is asking you to do.

I also want to say something about timing before we go any further. There is never a perfect moment to start building. The feed will always be crowded. Someone will always seem further ahead. The tools will always be changing. None of that is a reason to wait. The best time to start building an authentic brand was five years ago. The second best time is right now, today, with exactly what you have.

Who This Book Is For

I want to be specific about who I wrote this for, because I think it matters that you see yourself in these pages before we go any further.

This book is for you if you have been building for years and still feel like you are performing a version of yourself instead of actually being yourself. You have the following, you produce the content, you hit some of the numbers, and you still go to bed at night feeling like something is slightly off. Like the brand is close but not quite. Like you are almost saying what you actually mean but not all the way there yet. This book is for you.

It is for you if you built a business that looks successful from the outside but does not fully reflect who you are on the inside. You took every piece of advice about what the market wants and built toward that, and you are now standing in something that generates revenue but does not generate joy. This book is for you too.

It is for you if you have not started yet. You have the calling, you feel it clearly, and you have not moved on it because the fear is louder than the conviction right now. You have a thousand reasons why it is not the right time and a quiet knowing that most of those reasons are not actually reasons. This book was especially written for you.

And it is for you if you used to have something, a platform, a brand, a creative project, and walked away from it for whatever reason. Life, burnout, a season of doubt, a circumstance that required your full attention. And you are now wondering if it is too late to come back. I want to say clearly before we even begin: it is not. The calling does not expire. The gifts do not get recalled. You can pick this back up. This book will show you how.

What This Book Will and Will Not Do

I want to set honest expectations because I think you deserve that before you invest your time and your trust in these pages.

This book will not give you a content calendar. It will not tell you exactly how many times a week to post or which hashtags to use or what time of day the algorithm rewards. There are plenty of resources for that. What this book will do is far more foundational. It will help you understand who you are well enough that all of those tactical decisions become easier. Because when you know your voice, your values, your story, and your mission, the content decisions almost make themselves.

This book will not make building feel effortless. What it will do is make it feel meaningful. There is a difference between the grind of building something that is not aligned with who you are and the work of building something that is entirely, specifically, unmistakably yours. The second kind is still hard. But it is a different quality of hard. It is the kind of hard that fills you up instead of draining you. That is what we are building toward.

What this book will do is give you a framework that lasts. Platforms will change. Trends will shift. The landscape of the creator economy will look entirely different in five years than it does today. But the principles in this book are not platform-dependent. They are rooted in who you are, and who you are does not change with the algorithm. Build on that foundation and you will never have to start over. You will only have to evolve.

Let's dive in.

Authenticity Beyond the Screen

You do not have to be a content creator to live this.

Before we go any further, I want to make something clear. Because I think it is the most important thing I could say before you turn another page.

A lot of what you will find in these pages touches on building a brand in the digital world. Platforms, content, showing up online, making yourself visible. That is real and we are going there. But I need you to know from the jump that none of it is reserved for people who want to be content creators. This book is for anyone who wants to live and work as the most authentic version of themselves. That is a much bigger group than the internet would have you believe.

These principles work whether you are a content creator with a hundred thousand followers or a person who has never posted a single thing and has no desire to. Whether you are a nurse showing up for your patients with full presence and genuine care, a teacher who pours herself into a classroom of twenty-three kids, a small business owner in a town of five thousand people, or someone who just wants to move through the world as the most honest version of themselves. Authenticity is not a digital strategy. It is a way of being.

---

*You do not need a platform to be your most
authentic self. The platform is just one of
many places where that self can show up.*

These Principles Work Everywhere

Every principle in this book applies to your everyday life just as much as it applies to your content calendar. Knowing your gifts and building from them? That applies whether you are cleaning houses or closing deals or raising children or running a company. Staying true to your values when the pressure to compromise is real? That happens in boardrooms and breakrooms and family dinners. Showing up consistently as the same person in every room? That is just called integrity.

I have watched people apply these principles and never post a single piece of content. They just started showing up differently. More honestly. More confidently. More themselves. And things started shifting. Opportunities found them. Relationships deepened. Work became more fulfilling. Not because they built a brand online but because they stopped performing a version of themselves and started actually being themselves.

Proverbs 18:16 says a man's gift makes room for him and brings him before great men. The gift makes the room. Not the platform. Not the follower count. Not the aesthetic. The gift. Your job is simply to steward it faithfully, in every space you occupy.

This Is for Everyone

Maybe you picked up this book because you want to build something big. A brand. A business. A platform that reaches people all over the world. I am here for that. Let's go.

Maybe you picked it up because you are just trying to figure out who you are and how to show up as that person without apology. That is just as valid. That is just as important. That is honestly the foundation of everything else.

Or maybe you are somewhere in the middle. You have a life you love, a calling that drives you, and a quiet feeling that you want to share some of it. Not to build an empire. Just because you have something worth saying and the world might be better for hearing it. Go for it. That is enough of a reason. That has always been enough of a reason.

Being authentic paves the way for you to create anything you want. Or maybe you don't want to create anything. Maybe you are just inspired to share your life. That is more than enough. Go for it.

The Real Goal

I am not trying to turn everyone into a content creator. I am trying to help everyone find their gifts, understand what they are called to do, and go do it without shrinking, without performing, and without waiting for someone to give them permission.

Whether that looks like a YouTube channel or a quiet life of deep impact, whether it looks like a business that changes an industry or a career spent serving people in ways that never make headlines, whether it looks like something the world celebrates or something only the people closest to you ever see, it is yours. Build it authentically. Show up honestly. Let the gifts God placed in you do the work they were designed to do.

That is the whole thing. That has always been the whole thing.

How to Use This Book

This book is designed to be read straight through, but it does not have to be. Each Detail stands on its own and can be returned to whenever you need it most.

If you want to go deeper as you go, the Original By Design Companion Workbook gives you space to write, reflect, and build alongside every chapter. You do not need the workbook to get everything out of this book. But if you are ready to go all the way in, it is there for you.

Read with a pen in your hand. Come back to the pages that hit. Let this be a conversation, not a lecture. That is how it was written.

Detail 1: Discover Your Unique Talents

Your Superpower Is Already Within You

One of the biggest mistakes people make when building a brand is assuming they need to become something special first. But God already settled that question. He made you on purpose, with purpose.

Your personal brand is not something you manufacture. It is something you uncover. God placed it in you, in the way you think, the way you communicate, the way you naturally make people feel. Your job is not to invent it. It is to recognize it and have the courage to build from it.

Think about it. Have you ever noticed how certain things come effortlessly to you that seem to completely baffle other people? Maybe you have a way with words. Maybe you can walk into any room and instantly read the energy. Maybe you see solutions to problems before anyone else even notices there is a problem.

Those are not coincidences. Those are clues.

Jeremiah 1:5 says, 'Before I formed you in the womb I knew you.' That is not poetry. That is the foundation of everything in this book. Your uniqueness was not an accident. The things that light you up were placed there by a God who knew exactly what He was doing.

The Trap Most People Fall Into

Most people overlook their greatest talents precisely because they come so naturally. They assume, 'If this is easy for me, it must be easy for everyone.' So they dismiss their gifts as ordinary and spend years chasing someone else's version of extraordinary.

I have seen this pattern over and over again. A woman who can walk into a room and connect with every single person in it tells me she does not have any special skills. A man who can explain the most complex ideas in simple, beautiful language says he is not really a writer. A young entrepreneur who built a business from nothing at twenty-two says they were just lucky.

That is not luck. That is a gift. Own it.

How to Identify Your Gifts

1. Reflect on What Comes Effortlessly

- What do people always come to you for? What do they thank you for?
- What activities make hours feel like minutes?
- What could you teach someone without preparing at all?

Pay close attention to what others say about you. Sometimes it is easier for the people around us to see our gifts than it is for us to see them ourselves. If three different people have told you the same thing, believe them.

2. Look at Your Life for Patterns

Your whole life has been leaving clues. Your childhood interests, your hobbies, your work history, the things that kept pulling you back even when you tried to walk away. They all point somewhere.

Were you always the kid who organized your friend group? Leadership and connection are your gifts. Were you constantly writing in journals or narrating your own thoughts? Storytelling is your gift. Were you the person everyone called when they were falling apart? You have the gift of presence and wisdom.

3. Ask the People Closest to You

Send a message to five people who know you well. A friend, a family member, a former colleague. Ask them two questions:

- What do you think I am uniquely gifted at?
- What do you always come to me for?

The answers will likely surprise you. And they will tell you more about your brand potential than any quiz or personality test ever could.

Finding the Sweet Spot

The most powerful personal brands live at the intersection of three things:

- What you love doing (your passion)
- What you are naturally great at (your talent)
- What people need and will pay for (your market)

When all three align, you stop working in the traditional sense. You start living your purpose out loud. And there is nothing more magnetic than someone doing exactly what they were made to do.

Here is something I have noticed in every creator I have ever worked with or watched from a distance: the ones who break through are almost never the most technically skilled. They are the most specifically themselves. Their brand has a fingerprint on it that no one else could replicate, because it comes from a combination of talent, experience, and perspective that is completely unique to them. That fingerprint is what you are looking for. Not a niche. Not a category. A fingerprint.

So do not rush this part. Take the questions in this chapter seriously. Sit with them. The time you spend getting clear on your gifts before you start building is not time lost. It is the foundation everything else will stand on. A brand built on a clear understanding of your own gifts will outlast any trend, survive any algorithm change, and still be standing when every shortcut has run its course.

The Difference Between Good and Called

There is a distinction I want to draw before we close this chapter, because I think it is important. There is a difference between being good at something and being called to it. You can be skilled at things that are not yours to build a brand around. You can be competent at work that drains you. You can be impressive in spaces that do not align with who you actually are.

The goal of this chapter is not to identify what you are good at. It is to identify what is yours. Your gifts, in the deepest sense, are not just the things you can do well. They are the things that feel like home when you do them. The things that make you feel more alive, not less. The things that fill you up even when they are hard. That intersection of skill and aliveness is where your brand belongs.

Some people spend decades being excellent at the wrong things. Excellent by external standards, celebrated in rooms that do not reflect who they actually are, building careers that look impressive and feel hollow. I do not want that for you. I want you to build something that looks like you and feels like you and matters to you. That is a much higher standard than impressive, and it is absolutely achievable if you are willing to be honest in this chapter.

> *I believe God gives every person a specific assignment. Your brand is how you carry that assignment into the marketplace. It does not have to be a ministry. It can be a business, a platform, a product, a persona. What matters is that it is yours.*

Here is something I want you to sit with: the reason your gifts feel ordinary to you is because they are so deeply yours that you have forgotten they are not universal. The thing that feels like second nature to you is someone else's impossible. The way you see the world, the way you solve problems, the way you make people feel when you are in the room, those are not small things. Those are the exact things someone out there is desperately looking for.

This is why personal branding is not vanity. It is stewardship. When you build around the gifts God gave you and show up consistently, you are not promoting yourself. You are making yourself available to the people He meant for you to reach. The gifts were never just for you. They were always meant to serve someone.

I want to leave you with one more thought before we move on to building. The world already has plenty of people trying to be what the market wants. What it is actually short on is people willing to be fully, completely, without apology themselves. That is the scarcest and most valuable thing you can bring to any industry or audience. Not more strategy. More you. Start there and do not stop.

If You Are Starting From Zero

I want to speak directly to the person who is reading this with a blank page in front of them. No following. No brand. No content. Maybe not even a clear idea of what they want to build. Just a feeling that they were made for something more than what they are currently doing, and a book someone told them might help.

First: you are exactly where you need to be. The blank page is not a problem. It is the most honest starting point there is. You have not built anything in the wrong direction yet. You have not spent years speaking in someone else's voice. You have not tied your identity to metrics that do not reflect your actual calling. You are free in a way that people who have been building for years sometimes have to work hard to get back to. Do not underestimate that.

Second: starting from zero does not mean starting from nothing. You have a lifetime of experiences, a specific way of seeing the world, a set of gifts that have been operating in you long before you ever thought about building a brand. Zero followers does not mean zero foundation. The foundation is you. And you have been building that foundation your entire life without knowing it was for this.

Third: the people who build the most durable brands are often the ones who started with the most clarity about why they were doing it, not the most resources or the most head start. When you build from nothing, every decision is intentional. You do not have old habits to unlearn or a misaligned audience to slowly redirect. You get to build exactly the right thing from the very first post. That is not a disadvantage. That is a gift.

Here is what I want you to do before you move to the next chapter. Sit with this question honestly: if you could create anything, serve anyone, and be known for something, what would it be? Do not filter for what seems realistic or what the market seems to want right now. Just answer from the most honest part of yourself. Write it down. That answer is the seed of your brand. Everything in this book is about helping you grow it.

Jeremiah 29:11 says I know the plans I have for you, plans to prosper you and not to harm you, plans to give you hope and a future. That verse is not just for people who already have things figured out. It is specifically for the person standing at the beginning, looking out at a future they cannot fully see yet, wondering if there is something there for them. There is. Keep reading.

From Gift to Brand: Making the Connection

Here is where a lot of people get stuck. They do the work of identifying their gift, they fill out the exercises, they sit with the questions, they arrive at something that feels true, and then they stop. They hold the gift in their hands and they do not know what to do with it next. The gap between knowing your gift and building a brand around it can feel like crossing an ocean with no map.

I want to give you the bridge.

Your gift is not a niche. It is not a content strategy. It is not a product. It is the foundation beneath all of those things. The gift is the why. The brand is how that why shows up in the world in a way that other people can find, follow, and benefit from. When you understand that relationship, gift as foundation and brand as expression, everything about the building process becomes clearer.

Here is a practical way to think about it. Ask yourself three questions. First: what is the gift I identified in this chapter? Be specific. Not a category, an actual thing. Second: who is the person who most needs what that gift produces? Not everyone. One person. Describe them. Third: what does that person's life look like after they have encountered what I build? What changes for them? What becomes possible?

The answers to those three questions are the skeleton of your brand. The gift is what you bring. The person is who you bring it to. The transformation is why they will care. Everything else, the name, the visuals, the content, the offers, is just the brand putting clothes on that skeleton. And clothes can change. The skeleton stays.

This is why two people can have the same gift and build completely different brands. Two people with a gift for teaching might build entirely different platforms, serve entirely different audiences, and create entirely different kinds of impact, because the gift is not the whole story. The gift plus your specific story plus your specific audience plus your specific calling equals something that has never existed before. That is your brand. And that is why nobody can replicate it.

Your gift is the foundation. Your brand is how that gift shows up in the world in a way that people can find. Build from the foundation up. Everything else follows.

Proverbs 18:16 says a person's gift opens doors for them and brings them before great people. Notice what it does not say. It does not say a person's strategy opens doors. It does not say their aesthetic or their posting schedule or their growth hacks. The gift. The gift is what moves things. Your only job is to build something that lets the gift be seen. That is what the next several chapters are going to help you do.

Detail 2: Define Your Brand Identity

Become Magnetic

Now that you have uncovered what makes you special, it is time to build a clear, recognizable brand identity that people instantly connect with.

A strong personal brand does not happen by accident. It is intentional. It is built on consistency, clarity, and the courage to take up space.

1. Define Your Mission and Message

Your mission is the driving force behind your brand. It answers the single most important question: Why do you do what you do?

- What impact do you want to create in the world?

- Who do you most want to help?

- What do you want people to feel when they encounter your brand?

A strong mission statement is specific, values-driven, and human. It should feel less like a corporate tagline and more like something you would say to a friend over coffee.

2. Establish Your Core Values

Your values are the non-negotiables of your brand. They determine what you will and will not do, what you will and will not say yes to, and who you will and will not partner with.

- Authenticity: showing up as your full, unedited self
- Generosity: leading with giving before you ever ask
- Faith: trusting the process even when results are not visible yet
- Excellence: doing the work with intention and care
- Joy: refusing to build something that drains the life out of you

When your audience sees your values in action, consistently over time, they do not just follow you. They trust you. And trust is the currency of every successful brand.

> *Proverbs 11:3 says the integrity of the upright guides them. When your values are clear and you live them publicly, the right people find you and the wrong opportunities naturally fall away.*

3. Craft Your Brand Story

Your story is your most powerful marketing tool. The most counterintuitive truth about storytelling is this: your struggles are more valuable than your successes.

People do not connect with the highlight reel. They connect with the moment before the breakthrough. The 'I almost gave up' moment. The 'nobody believed in me' moment. The 'I had no idea what I was doing' moment.

A great brand story has four parts:

- Where you started (your origin, your before)

- What you faced (the challenge, the doubt, the no)

- What you discovered (the turning point, the lesson, the shift)

- Where you are now, and how you want to take others there too

Notice what is not on that list: credentials. Impressive titles. A perfectly linear path. The things that make a brand story powerful are not the polished parts. They are the human parts. The moment you almost quit. The season when nothing was working. The thing you had to unlearn before you could grow. Those are the parts of your story that make someone reading it think, that sounds exactly like where I am right now. And the moment someone thinks that, you have their full attention.

Your story does not have to be dramatic to be powerful. You do not need to have survived something extraordinary. You just need to be honest about something real. A quiet story told with complete honesty will always land harder than a dramatic story told with even the slightest hint of performance. Tell the true version. Every time.

4. Develop Your Visual and Verbal Identity

Once you know who you are and what you stand for, the visual and verbal layers of your brand should simply reflect that truth outward.

- Your color palette and design aesthetic: choose what feels genuinely like you, not what is trending
- Your tone of voice: playful? warm? bold? scholarly? Let your natural voice lead
- Your content style: long-form writing, short videos, podcasting, community. Play to your strengths

Consistency across these elements is what makes a brand recognizable. You do not have to be everywhere. You just have to be consistently, undeniably yourself wherever you are.

Here is something most brand guides skip entirely: the version of you that God made, including the specific humor, the particular perspective, the opinions that might make some people uncomfortable, that is not a liability to be managed. That is the asset. The world already has polished and filtered. What it does not have is another you.

The brands that last are not the most generic. They are the most specific. The more clearly you can articulate who you are and what you stand for, the more powerfully your brand will attract the people who were always meant to be in your world.

One of the most common mistakes people make at this stage is building a brand identity that reflects who they think they should be rather than who they actually are. They look at what is working for someone else, what colors are trending, what tone seems to be performing, and they build toward that. And then they wonder why the brand feels hollow to them, why they cannot stay consistent, why it does not feel like theirs.

Your brand identity should feel like a relief when you land on it. Not a costume you put on, but a mirror you finally cleaned. When your visual identity, your tone of voice, and your core message are genuinely aligned with who you are, showing up consistently stops feeling like discipline and starts feeling like second nature. That is the target. Not perfection. Alignment.

Case Study: Jaclynn Belts

What happens when passion is the strategy

Before I walk you through the framework of building an authentic brand, I want to show you what it looks like in practice. Not with someone famous. Not with a polished success story. With something I built myself, from scratch, for the pure love of it.

Jaclynn Belts is a persona I created. A music project. A brand built around performance, creativity, and the joy of doing something I genuinely loved, even though nobody asked me to and even though, by every conventional measure, I was not the obvious candidate to do it.

Let me be direct: singing was not my claimed professional expertise. I was not a trained vocalist. I had not won competitions or been signed to a label or been told by industry gatekeepers that I had what it takes. By the world's standards, there were a hundred reasons not to do it.

I did it anyway. And that decision turned into one of the most genuinely fun and creatively rewarding things I have ever done.

It Started With Fun

When I started Jaclynn Belts, I was not thinking about strategy. I was not calculating reach or analyzing trends or building toward a monetization plan. I was just leaning into the fun of it. That was the whole point. To create something expressive and real and mine, without the weight of needing it to perform.

That might sound simple, but I want you to understand how important that was. The lightness I brought to it was not naivety. It was intentional. I gave myself permission to enjoy the process before I ever asked the process to deliver results. And that freedom is what made everything that came after possible.

What I had was passion. A clear point of view. A willingness to show up. And the conviction that those things were enough to build something worth paying attention to.

The Beginning Was Quiet

I want to be honest with you about something that does not always make it into the success story version of things: in the beginning, it did not take off. The audience was small. The reach was limited. There were posts that went nowhere and moments where the silence on the other end could have felt discouraging.

But I stayed consistent. Not because the numbers were rewarding me. Because the work itself was. Because every time I showed up, I was doing something that felt true. And I had learned enough by then to know that the compound interest of consistency always pays out eventually. You just have to keep making deposits even when the balance looks low.

So that is what I did. I kept showing up. The same energy, the same voice, the same joy that started it. Not performing consistency, actually living it. Month after month, quietly building something that was entirely and unapologetically itself.

Romans 11:29 says the gifts and calling of God are irrevocable. I kept coming back to that through the slow season. The door the industry wanted to close was never the door I needed to walk through anyway.

And Then One Day, Everything Changed

I cannot point to a single viral moment or a campaign that flipped a switch. What I can tell you is that one day the audience was there. Not all at once, but undeniably. People who had been watching quietly started engaging. The community that had been forming in the background became visible. The work I had been doing consistently in private started bearing fruit publicly.

That is how it usually happens. Not in a dramatic announcement. In a quiet shift. You look up one day and realize that what you have been building is actually standing. The audience found the brand because the brand was always, consistently, genuinely there.

It became monetizable. A real business emerged from a project that started as creative passion. Content, merchandise, partnerships. The kind of thing people told me would not work without the right credentials became something that worked precisely because it was not trying to be anything other than what it was.

What It Looks Like Now

Here is the part of the story I want you to sit with: I do not post every day. I never have. And Jaclynn Belts is still here, still alive, still a community that shows up when I do.

That is what building from passion instead of pressure actually looks like in practice. I come back when I have something real to share. When the creative energy is there. When it feels true. And when I do show up, the community is there too. Not because I have been performing consistency, but because the connection we built is genuine enough that it does not require constant maintenance to stay real.

The narrative around building a brand online is almost always about volume. Post more. Show up more. Be everywhere. And I want to tell you that is not the whole truth. When a brand is built on authenticity, when the people who follow you actually know who you are and why you do what you do, you earn something no algorithm can manufacture: trust that does not expire between posts.

My community knows me. They know my voice, my values, what I care about. They know what it feels like when I show up. So when I come back after a quiet season, they are not questioning whether I am still committed. They are not wondering if the brand changed. They just know it is me, and they are glad I am back. That is the difference between building followers and building people. Followers need content. People need connection.

And here is what that has made possible: I get to share when it is genuine. I get to create from a full place instead of an obligated one. I built something I can come back to on my own terms because I built it around who I actually am. The community is not waiting on a schedule. They are waiting on me. And that is only possible because I never tried to be anything other than myself in the first place.

---

*You do not have to be the best at something
to build something special from it. You just
have to trust what God placed in you
enough to actually use it.*

The Case Study Takeaway

Here is what Jaclynn Belts demonstrates, in practical terms, about authentic brand building:

Start with joy. If you are not enjoying what you are building, your audience will feel that too. The energy you bring to the work is part of the brand.

Stay consistent when no one is watching. The quiet seasons are where the foundation gets laid. Do not let low numbers in the beginning convince you that nothing is happening. Something is always happening beneath the surface of consistent effort.

Trust the turning point. It will come. Not on your timeline, but it will come. Keep showing up and let God handle the timing.

Build something sustainable. The goal is not to post the most. The goal is to build something so rooted in who you are that it can stand on its own, serve your audience deeply, and still leave room for you to be a whole person outside of it.

Jaclynn Belts gave me proof. Proof that passion is a strategy. That consistency is a superpower. That authenticity compounds. And that proof became the foundation of everything I went on to build. What you build from your gifts will do the same for you.

The permission you are waiting for is not coming from the industry, the critics, or the market. It was already given. God gave you the gift. That is the permission. When He places something in you, He is not waiting for a panel of judges to approve it. The call is the credential.

Start. Stay consistent. Trust the process. And on the days when the numbers are quiet, remember: you are not building for the algorithm. You are building for the people God meant for you to reach. They are coming. Keep building.

Detail 3: Show Up and Own Your Space

Build Trust and Visibility

You have identified your gifts. You have defined your brand. You have crafted your story. Now comes the part that most people skip, delay, or talk themselves out of.

You have to show up.

A brand that lives only in your head is not a brand. It is a dream. And there is a crucial difference between the two. Dreams are beautiful and necessary, but they do not create income, impact, or community on their own. Action does.

The biggest mistake you can make in building your personal brand is hiding.

I know the fear. I have lived it. What if people judge me? What if nobody cares? What if I put myself out there and it does not work? What if I am not ready yet?

Here is the hard truth I had to learn: you will never feel ready. Readiness is not a feeling that arrives before you start. It is a feeling that develops because you started. The only way out is through. Through begins with showing up.

> *Matthew 5:15 says you do not light a lamp and put it under a bowl. You put it on a stand so it gives light to everyone in the house. Your gift is the lamp. Visibility is the stand. Do not dim your own light out of fear.*

Choosing Your Platform

- If you love to write, a newsletter, a blog, or LinkedIn is your playground.

- If you light up on camera, YouTube, TikTok, or Instagram Reels is where you belong.

- If your gift is conversation and connection, a podcast or live community is your stage.

- If you are deeply analytical or educational, long-form content, courses, or in-depth guides suit you.

The platform should serve your gift, not the other way around. I see too many people forcing themselves onto platforms that drain them because it is trendy, and then wondering why they cannot stay consistent. Consistency is easy when you are doing what comes naturally.

Be Relatable: People Follow People, Not Personas

The things that make you human, your learning curve, your behind-the-scenes moments, your honest reflections, your pivots and corrections, those are not weaknesses. They are the connective tissue of your brand. They are the reason someone who does not know you will decide to trust you.

Create Content That Actually Serves People

Every piece of content you create should do at least one of three things: teach something, inspire something, or make someone feel seen. When your content does any one of those things consistently, you do not just build an audience. You build a community of people who genuinely need what you offer.

- Answer the questions your audience is already asking.

- Share the lessons you wish someone had given you earlier.

- Be the voice you needed when you were starting out.

Engage Like a Human Being

A brand is not a broadcast. It is a conversation. I would rather have a thousand people who feel deeply connected to what I am building than a million passive scrollers. Depth beats breadth every time.

God did not design us to broadcast. He designed us for relationship. The brands that last are not built on followers. They are built on genuine human connection, one person at a time.

Showing up consistently is hard. I will not pretend otherwise. There will be days when you do not feel like it, when the numbers feel discouraging, when you wonder if any of it is working. Those are the days that actually build the brand. Anyone can show up when it is going well. The creators who build something lasting are the ones who show up anyway, on the quiet days, on the days without engagement, on the days when the only reason to create is because they know it is theirs to do.

Think of consistency like planting. Each time you show up, you are sowing something. It may not look like much in the moment. But God grows what we faithfully plant. Over time, those seeds become something that nobody can replicate, because nobody else carries your voice, your story, your specific assignment. That harvest is built through faithfulness, not force. Plant now. Keep going.

I also want to say something about consistency, because I think it is one of the most misunderstood words in personal branding. Consistency does not mean posting every day. It does not mean never taking a break or never having an off week. It means that when you show up, people recognize you. Your voice, your values, your perspective are stable enough that your audience always knows what they are getting. That kind of consistency is built slowly, not through volume, but through integrity.

And here is the thing about showing up before you feel ready: the feedback you get from actually being visible is worth more than any amount of time spent preparing in private. Your audience will teach you things about your brand that you could never learn sitting alone with your ideas. The market responds to what is real. Go find out what is real about you by putting it in front of people and paying close attention to what lands.

Building a Sustainable Content Rhythm

I want to give you something practical before we talk about the hard seasons, because I think one of the biggest reasons creators burn out is not lack of passion. It is lack of structure. And I do not mean a rigid content calendar with color-coded posting schedules. I mean a simple, honest framework for how you show up that you can actually sustain over time without destroying yourself.

Here is what sustainable rhythm actually looks like in practice. It starts with deciding your non-negotiable frequency. Not what the algorithm rewards, not what the most successful person in your space does, but what you can genuinely commit to without resentment. For some people that is five times a week. For others it is twice. There is no right answer. The only wrong answer is promising yourself and your audience something you cannot maintain, because inconsistency is far more damaging to a brand than a slower posting schedule.

Once you know your frequency, build your rhythm around your actual life, not an idealized version of it. If you have the most creative energy on Tuesday mornings, that is your creation window. If Friday afternoons are when everything falls apart, that is not the time to try to write something meaningful. Your content rhythm should fit into the life you actually have, not require a life you do not.

The Content Bank

One of the most practical things you can do for your brand is build a content bank. This is simply a document, a note, a folder, some place where you collect ideas before you need them. A thought that surfaced during a walk. A question someone asked you that you realized you had a lot to say about. A frustration in your industry that nobody seems to be addressing honestly. A story from your own journey that you keep coming back to.

Most creators wait until it is time to post to figure out what to say. And then they sit down with a blank screen and the pressure of the posting deadline and they create something that is fine but not great. The content bank solves this. When you capture ideas consistently in real time, when the inspiration actually hits, you always have something real to draw from. You are not manufacturing content under pressure. You are selecting from a bank of things that already mattered to you.

Keep this bank simple. A note in your phone works perfectly. The goal is not organization. The goal is capture. Ideas are slippery. They feel like they will still be there later and then they are not. The two minutes it takes to write something down when it occurs to you is one of the highest-return investments you can make in your content life.

Batching and Breathing

Another tool worth building into your rhythm is batching. This means setting aside dedicated time to create multiple pieces of content at once rather than trying to create something new every single day. Many creators find that their creative energy runs higher on some days than others. Batching lets you capitalize on the high-energy days to cover the lower ones.

The goal is not to create content that feels manufactured or stockpiled. It is to separate the creative act from the publishing deadline so that neither one is poisoned by the other. When you create without a posting deadline looming over you, you tend to create better. When you publish from a place of surplus rather than scarcity, you tend to show up with more confidence. Build a system that gives you both.

And build breathing room into the system. Leave weeks in the calendar where you are not expected to produce anything new. Treat those weeks as investment weeks. Read something that inspires you. Have a conversation that fills you up. Experience something outside your usual frame of reference. Your audience will receive the content that comes after those weeks at a noticeably higher level. Breathing is not a retreat from your brand. It is part of building it.

When Showing Up Gets Hard

There will be seasons when showing up feels genuinely hard. Not just uncomfortable, but heavy. Seasons when you have poured a lot out and the results feel slow. Seasons when the criticism lands harder than usual. Seasons when you look at what you have built and wonder if it is working or if it matters or if anyone is actually paying attention.

Those seasons are not signs that you should stop. They are signs that you are in the middle, and the middle is the hardest part of any meaningful journey. The beginning has momentum and excitement. The end has the satisfaction of completion. The middle has neither. It is just the daily decision to keep going, on days when the evidence for keeping going is thin.

Here is what I have learned about getting through the middle: shrink the target. Instead of asking yourself whether the whole vision is working, ask yourself whether you can show up today. Just today. Post the one thing. Make the one connection. Write the one paragraph. When the big picture feels overwhelming, the day-sized target is almost always manageable. And enough days strung together always become something.

> *Psalm 37:5 says commit your way to the Lord, trust in Him, and He will act. I have clung to that in the hard seasons of building. You do not have to figure out the whole path. You have to commit what is in front of you and trust that the next step will become clear when you get there. It always has.*

Detail 4: Monetize Your Authentic Brand

Get Paid for Being You

Let us talk about money. Because I know this is where a lot of people start to get uncomfortable. There is a conditioning many of us carry that says talking about what you have built, or asking to be paid well for it, is somehow arrogant. I want to address that directly.

I need you to hear this clearly: being paid for what you are gifted at is not greedy. It is not selling out. It is not unspiritual. It is the natural outcome of providing real value to real people. And it is how you make your work sustainable.

Deuteronomy 8:18 reminds us that it is God who gives us the ability to produce wealth. He does not give you a gift and then expect you to apologize for using it. You are allowed to prosper from what He placed inside you.

With Jaclynn Belts, I did not wait until I had a record deal or a million followers to start making money. I built a brand, showed up consistently, provided value. Then I created offerings that my audience actually needed. That is the sequence. And it works.

Ways to Monetize Your Personal Brand

1. Digital Products and Courses

If you have knowledge or a skill that someone else needs, you can package it. An e-book, a mini-course, a workshop, a template pack. Digital products are low overhead and highly scalable.

2. Coaching and Consulting

Your lived experience has value. People are willing to pay to shortcut their learning curve. You just need to be further along than the person you are helping.

3. Affiliate Marketing and Partnerships

Recommending products and services you genuinely use and love, and earning a commission when your audience purchases them, is one of the most authentic monetization strategies available. The key word is genuinely. Your audience trusts you. Never trade that trust for a quick check.

4. Brand Collaborations and Sponsorships

As your brand grows, companies will want access to your audience. Long-term partnerships built on shared mission are far more valuable, financially and reputationally, than one-off promotional posts.

5. Speaking Engagements and Live Events

If you have a powerful message and the courage to deliver it from a stage, in person or virtually, speaking is one of the most lucrative and impactful ways to monetize your brand. One keynote can open ten doors.

6. Memberships and Subscriptions

If you create consistent, high-value content, a paid membership or subscription model lets your most dedicated fans support your work directly while receiving exclusive access in return. This creates recurring revenue and deepens community at the same time.

One thing I want to address directly: the fear of charging what you are worth. This shows up for almost everyone. The belief that asking for money somehow diminishes the authenticity of what you are doing. That if you really cared, you would give it away.

Here is what I know to be true: you cannot sustain what you cannot fund. A brand built entirely on free content with no revenue model is not a business. It is a hobby with an audience. And there is nothing wrong with hobbies. But if your calling is to build something that creates lasting impact, that serves people at scale, that grows beyond what you can do alone, then you need a sustainable financial foundation. Charging for your expertise is not greed. It is stewardship.

The Revenue Funnel

You do not build trust and then ask for money. You build trust, keep building trust, and eventually your audience is so clear on the value you provide that the invitation to go deeper is a natural next step, not a pitch.

1. Provide free value first. Teach, inspire, serve. Give before you ever ask.

2. Convert followers to subscribers. Give them a reason to stay close.

3. Nurture consistently. Show up. Keep delivering. Keep being you.

4. Make the offer. Let people see clearly how your product or service solves a real problem they already have.

Luke 6:38 says give and it will be given to you. The most successful brands I know are obsessively generous. They give so much value for free that when they do make an offer, people feel like they are still getting a deal.

Something I want to name specifically: pricing your work is an act of self-respect. I have watched talented people chronically underprice what they offer because they are not sure they are worth more. But your price is not just a reflection of what something costs to produce. It is a signal of the value your audience can expect to receive. When you charge what your work is actually worth, you attract people who take it seriously. And you give yourself the resources to keep doing the work at a level you are proud of.

Start somewhere. You do not need to have the perfect offer, the perfect price point, or the perfect funnel before you begin. You need to understand your audience, know what they need, and make them a genuine offer that delivers real value. Everything else can be refined over time. The brands that figure out monetization are the ones that start, pay attention, and adjust. Not the ones that plan the longest.

One of the most liberating things I ever learned about monetization is that your first offer does not have to be your best offer. It just has to be honest. Make a real promise and deliver on it completely. Do that consistently and your audience's trust compounds. Their trust is your actual asset. Money is just what happens when trust meets a relevant offer. Protect the trust. Everything else grows from there.

On Charging What You Are Worth

I want to address something directly because it comes up in almost every conversation I have with creators about money: the discomfort of charging what your work is actually worth.

Many of us have internalized the message that wanting to be well-compensated for creative work is somehow greedy or ungrateful. I want to name that message clearly so we can put it down. It is not truth. It is conditioning.

You are allowed to be paid well for work that is genuinely excellent. You are allowed to raise your prices as your skills and your audience grow. You are allowed to say no to opportunities that underpay you even when the exposure sounds appealing. Every time you accept less than your work is worth, you are sending a signal to the market about your value. And the market believes you. So start telling it the truth.

Know Your Number Before They Call

One of the most powerful things you can do before monetization gets real is decide, in advance, what you will not accept. Not in a rigid way that leaves no room for relationship or context, but in a grounded way that means you are never making a financial decision from a place of desperation or flattery.

Decide what your minimum rate is. Decide what kind of brands you will not work with regardless of the number. Decide what your time is worth per hour when you account for all the invisible labor, the emails, the prep, the creative thinking, that surrounds any deliverable. Write those things down before the offer comes. Because when the offer comes with a number attached and a deadline and a compliment about how perfect you would be for this, your clarity will be tested. The creators who hold their standard are the ones who decided what that standard was before they were in the room.

And I want to say something about the low offer that comes wrapped in prestige. The unpaid feature in a major publication. The small fee for a high-profile event. The brand deal with a name everyone recognizes that pays a fraction of your rate. Prestige is not a business model. Exposure does not pay your rent. You can honor the opportunity and still ask to be paid appropriately for it. Those two things are not in conflict. The brands and outlets that genuinely respect you will not disappear when you ask to be compensated fairly. The ones that do were not going to serve your career the way they seemed to anyway.

Detail 5: The Art of Adaptation

Stay True While Evolving

Here is a tension every personal brand builder eventually faces: the pull between staying consistent and the natural desire to grow and change.

I want to tell you clearly: these are not opposites. You can evolve deeply without losing yourself. In fact, the most powerful brands do exactly that. They evolve in alignment with who they are becoming, not in reaction to what the market is doing.

A brand that stays stagnant risks becoming irrelevant. A brand that changes too much loses its soul. The art is in growing while staying rooted.

Think of Your Brand Like a Tree

The roots of your brand, your core values, your mission, your authentic voice, those do not change. They deepen. They go further down as you grow further up. But the branches? The branches move. They spread into new directions. They try new things. They shed what no longer serves them and grow new ones.

Love her or hate her, Taylor Swift is one of the clearest brand case studies of our time. She started as a teenager writing country songs about heartbreak in small-town Tennessee. She is now one of the most powerful cultural forces on the planet, selling out stadiums in every genre she touches. But through every reinvention, she has never stopped being recognizably Taylor. Whatever you think of her music, the brand lesson is undeniable: the roots held.

I want to give you practical permission to change. Not permission to chase every trend or pivot every six months based on what the algorithm rewards. But real, grounded permission to grow into a fuller version of who you are and let your brand reflect that growth.

When you started, you could only build from who you were then. But you are not the same person you were when you began. Your perspective has deepened. Your experience has expanded. Your understanding of what you are actually called to do has probably sharpened considerably. Let your brand grow with you. The audience that was drawn to your authentic beginning will follow an authentic evolution. What they will not follow is a performance. Stay real, and you can become anything.

I think about Jaclynn Belts the same way. The brand evolved as I evolved. New offerings, new directions, new platforms. But the core of it, the unapologetic passion and authenticity at the center, never moved. That core is the thing people trust. Do not trade it for trends.

What My Own Evolution Actually Looked Like

Can I be real with you for a second? When I started evolving my brand, it was not graceful. I did not sit down one day with a vision board and a ten-step pivot plan and execute it beautifully. It was more like I kept noticing that certain things I was doing did not feel like me anymore and I did not have the language for why. The content was fine. The engagement was fine. But I would finish creating something and feel absolutely nothing. No satisfaction. No excitement. Just done.

That feeling is a signal, by the way. If you have ever finished a piece of content and felt completely empty about it, that is not a creative block. That is your brand trying to tell you something has grown out of alignment. Listen to that.

For me, the evolution was about going deeper, not broader. I had been showing up in a way that was true but not fully true. Like I was sharing the highlight version of my perspective instead of the whole thing. And at some point I just got tired of the highlight version. I wanted to say the thing I actually thought, in the way I actually thought it, without softening the edges so much that the point got lost.

So I started doing that. And honestly? It was terrifying for about a week and then it was the most freeing thing I had ever done. The people who had been there from the beginning loved it. Some people left. That is fine. The ones who stayed were exactly who I was supposed to be talking to. And the ones who found me after the shift were an even more aligned community than I had before.

That is what evolution in alignment looks like. You do not lose yourself. You find more of yourself. And the brand gets sharper, more specific, more undeniably you. Which, as we have established, is the whole point.

How to Evolve Without Losing Yourself

- Check in with your core mission every six months. Ask yourself: am I still aligned with the impact I set out to create?

- Pay attention to your audience, but do not be controlled by them. Adapt to serve them better, but stay true to your own vision.

- Try new formats, new platforms, new offerings. But carry your voice with you into each one.

- Invest in yourself continuously. Read. Take courses. Find mentors. The version of you that existed when you started this brand is not the ceiling.

Philippians 1:6 says He who began a good work in you will carry it on to completion. Your brand is not finished. You are not finished. What has been started in you is still unfolding. The best chapters are often the ones that come after the hardest seasons.

One more thing worth saying about adaptation: do not confuse pivoting with quitting. Sometimes the most faithful thing you can do for your brand is change direction. Not because you failed, not because the original vision was wrong, but because you have grown into a clearer understanding of what you are actually called to do. That kind of pivot is not retreat. It is refinement. The difference is in the reason. Are you running away from something, or running toward something truer? One is fear. The other is growth.

The brands that navigate adaptation well are the ones that stay deeply anchored to their why even as their what evolves. Your mission is the compass. Your methods are just the vehicle. When the vehicle needs to change, change it. The compass stays.

I also want to give you permission to let things go. Part of evolving well is being willing to release what no longer serves you, old content pillars, old aesthetic choices, old ways of showing up that felt right two years ago but feel restrictive now. Letting something go is not a betrayal of your brand. It is part of growing it. Your audience will not be confused by your evolution if you bring them along with transparency. In fact, watching you grow in real time is often one of the most compelling things about following someone who builds authentically.

Coming Back After a Gap

I want to speak directly to the person who had something, walked away, and is now wondering if they can come back. Maybe life happened in a way that required all of your attention. A health crisis. A loss. A season of burnout so complete that the idea of creating anything felt impossible. A personal situation that made being visible feel unsafe or unwise. Whatever it was, you stepped away. And now some part of you is wondering if the door is still open.

It is. Let me say that as clearly as I can. The door is still open.

The gap does not erase what you built. It does not disqualify you from continuing. It does not mean your audience has forgotten you or that you have to start over from the beginning. What it means is that you get to come back with more to say than when you left. Every experience you had in the time away, even the hard ones, especially the hard ones, has given you material. It has deepened your perspective. It has made you more human, and being more human makes your brand more powerful, not less.

Here is what I have observed about creators who come back after a real gap: the ones who try to pretend the gap did not happen struggle. They come back and pick up where they left off as if nothing occurred, and their audience can feel the distance in it. But the ones who come back honestly, who acknowledge that they were away and share something real about the season they went through, they often come back to more engagement, more connection, and more loyalty than they had before they left. Because the return itself becomes a moment. And authenticity in the return, like authenticity everywhere else in this work, draws people in.

You do not owe anyone an explanation for why you were gone. But if you choose to share something real about it, your community will receive it. They have been waiting for you. Not for the content. For you.

How to Come Back Well

- Start smaller than you think you need to. One piece of content. One honest post. You do not have to come back at full volume to come back with full authenticity.

- Do not try to compensate for the gap with volume. Flooding your platform to make up for lost time will feel off to your audience and exhausting to you. Quality over pace.

- Give yourself grace for the first few pieces being imperfect. You are finding your voice again. That is allowed. It does not have to be perfect to be valuable.

- Reconnect with your why before you reconnect with your strategy. Sit with the reason you built this in the first place. Let that be what pulls you forward, not the pressure to perform.

- Tell your community something true. It does not have to be everything. But give them something real to hold. They will meet you there.

Isaiah 40:31 says those who wait on the Lord will renew their strength. They will soar on wings like eagles. They will run and not grow weary, they will walk and not be faint. The season away was not wasted. God was working in it. Come back from that place. Come back renewed. The people who need what you carry have been waiting for you.

Detail 6: There Is No Such Thing as Failure

It's All Part of the Story

Let me be honest with you about something: I have failed. Publicly, privately, expensively, and embarrassingly. I have launched things that did not land. I have made investments that did not pan out. I have created content that was met with silence so loud it felt like a verdict.

And here I am, still building. Still showing up. Still believing in what I was called to do.

Because I learned, slowly and sometimes painfully, that failure is not a stop sign. It is a detour. And detours often take you somewhere better than the original road would have.

Every so-called failure is just data dressed up in disappointment. Your only job is to learn from it and keep going.

Reframing What Failure Actually Means

A post that got no engagement? Now you know more about what your audience responds to.

A product launch that underwhelmed? Now you understand what to test differently, what message to sharpen, what offer to refine.

A partnership that fell apart? Now you have clearer criteria for who you do and do not align with.

None of these are endings. They are all information. And information, in the hands of someone committed to their purpose, is power.

Romans 8:28 says all things work together for good for those who love God and are called according to His purpose. I have watched this be true in my own life. The things that looked like failures often turned out to be redirections toward something better than what I originally planned.

The Stories That Keep Me Going

When I am tempted to quit, and yes there are days, I come back to the stories of people who did not.

J.K. Rowling was a single mother on welfare when she was writing Harry Potter. The manuscript was rejected by twelve publishers before Bloomsbury gave it a chance. The most successful book series in history almost did not exist because someone almost gave up.

Tyler Perry was homeless and living in his car when he staged his first play. It bombed. He staged it again. It bombed again. He kept going, for years, before Madea became a household name and he became one of the most successful independent filmmakers in Hollywood history.

Steve Jobs was fired from Apple, the company he founded. He described it later as the best thing that ever happened to him. It freed him to build Pixar and NeXT, and ultimately led to his return to Apple where he created the iPhone, the iPod, and the MacBook.

I want to say something about the silence. Because in brand building, there is a lot of it. You post something you are genuinely proud of and the response is underwhelming. You launch something you have been working on for months and the numbers do not reflect what you put in. You keep showing up and it feels like you are shouting into an empty room.

That silence is not a verdict. It is a season. Every significant brand I have ever watched grow went through a long, quiet period where nothing seemed to be working and the founder kept going anyway. The tipping point, when it comes, rarely announces itself in advance. You do not know you are one post away from the thing that changes everything. You just have to keep making the post. Keep doing the work. Keep being so consistently, undeniably yourself that when the right person finally finds you, they cannot look away.

None of these people were protected from failure. They were preserved through it. That is the difference.

What to Do When You Want to Quit

Okay. Real talk. Because I think this section deserves more than a list of tips.

There are going to be days when you want to pack it up. Close the account. Delete everything. Tell yourself it was a nice idea but maybe it was not for you. I know because I have had those days. And I know because almost every creator I have ever been close to has had those days too. The ones who look completely unbothered online. Them too. Especially them.

The day you want to quit usually does not come after a string of bad days. It comes after a long stretch of okay days that slowly drained something out of you without you fully noticing. You look up and you are tired in a way that sleep does not fix. You feel behind in a way that extra work does not solve. You are doing all the right things and feeling none of the right feelings. And quitting starts to sound less like giving up and more like relief.

Here is what I want you to do on that day. Not a list. Just one thing. Go find the reason you started. Not your strategy document. Not your content pillars. The actual reason. The feeling you had before you knew what any of this was supposed to look like. The person you wanted to help. The thing you wanted to say. The version of yourself you were building toward. Find that. Sit with it. Let it remind you that the tired you are feeling right now is not evidence that you were wrong to start. It is evidence that you have been pouring out. And people who are pouring out need to be refilled, not stopped.

Also, can I say something a little unpopular? Sometimes what feels like wanting to quit is actually just wanting a break. And those are not the same thing. We have this idea that real commitment means never wanting to stop. But that is not commitment. That is performance. Real commitment includes the hard days. It includes the days where you need to step back, breathe, and come back tomorrow. You are allowed to do that without calling it quitting. Taking a breath is not surrender. It is strategy.

And if you are truly in a season of deep doubt where everything you built feels shaky and you genuinely cannot see the point, talk to someone. Not your phone. An actual person who knows you and believes in what you are building. Sometimes all it takes is someone who sees what you cannot see right now to remind you that you are closer than you think. You do not have to carry the doubt alone. You were never supposed to.

> *Galatians 6:9 says do not grow weary in doing good, for at the proper time you will reap a harvest if you do not give up. The harvest is coming. Do not walk away from your field.*

I also want to say something about the timeline. We live in a culture that celebrates overnight success and rarely shows the years of quiet, unglamorous work that came before the breakthrough moment. The stories you heard earlier in this chapter, J.K. Rowling, Tyler Perry, Steve Jobs, did not make the news when they were failing. They made the news when they broke through. Which means you are getting a heavily edited version of every success story you admire. The real version almost always includes far more time, far more struggle, and far more doubt than the highlight reel suggests.

Give yourself the gift of a realistic timeline. Give yourself permission to still be building three years from now without deciding that means you are failing. Some of the most important brands in the world took a decade to find their audience. You are not behind. You are building. There is a difference.

I also want to challenge the way we talk about failure altogether. We say things like 'I failed' as though it is a permanent state, a label that sticks. But failure is just a moment in time. It is a single data point in a long experiment. The only way failure becomes final is if you stop experimenting. As long as you keep showing up, keep adjusting, and keep moving toward your calling, no single failure defines you. What defines you is the trajectory, and you get to keep shaping that every day you choose to keep going.

Bonus: The Inner Work of Branding

What No One Talks About

Most branding books will give you a strategy. A framework. A content calendar template. And those things have their place.

But nobody talks about what is actually the hardest part of building a personal brand: doing the inner work to believe you deserve a platform in the first place.

Imposter syndrome is real. The fear of being seen is real. The deep-seated belief that other people are more qualified, more talented, more worthy of attention. That is real. And if you do not address it, it will quietly sabotage everything you try to build.

The Comparison Trap

Social media was designed to show you other people's highlights. When you compare your beginning to someone else's middle, you will always feel behind. You will always feel like less than. And you will make decisions from that place of scarcity that will keep you small.

The only person you are supposed to be in competition with is the version of yourself from six months ago. Is that person still ahead of you? Then you have work to do. Is that person behind you? Then you are moving. Keep going.

God did not give you someone else's assignment. He gave you yours. Comparison is a distraction from your own purpose. Every moment you spend looking sideways is a moment you are not moving forward.

Dealing with Criticism

When you build a personal brand, you become visible. And visibility invites opinion. Some of that opinion will be supportive and life-giving. Some of it will be unkind, unfair, and personal.

Here is what I have learned about critics: the people most aggressively opposed to your audacity to show up are usually the people most afraid to show up themselves. That is not an insult. It is a truth. And it helps me not take it personally.

Not every piece of feedback deserves your attention. There is a difference between criticism from someone invested in your growth and noise from someone invested in their own comfort. Learn to tell the difference.

I want to leave you with this as we close out the inner work chapter: the most powerful thing you can do for your brand is become genuinely secure in who you are. Not arrogant. Not closed to growth. Secure. The kind of secure that lets you receive criticism without collapsing and praise without inflating. The kind of secure that lets you stay in your lane without resentment when someone else is thriving. The kind of secure that lets you keep building on the quiet days because you are not doing it for the applause.

That security does not come from success. It does not come from hitting a follower milestone or landing a big partnership. It comes from knowing whose you are. When your identity is rooted in what God says about you rather than what the metrics say about you, the whole game changes. Work on that relationship alongside the strategy. It will take you further than any tactic ever could.

Building a Brand Requires a Healthy Identity

Your brand is an expression of who you are, but it is not all of who you are. This is a critical distinction.

When a post underperforms, that is not a verdict on your worth. When a launch does not hit its numbers, that is not evidence that you do not belong here. When someone unfollows you, they are not rejecting you as a person. They are simply self-selecting out of your community.

Do the inner work alongside the outer work. Journal. Pray. Talk to a therapist or a coach. Build community with people who are doing the same hard thing. You cannot pour from empty, and you cannot build from a depleted self.

> *Your identity is not in your brand. Your brand flows from your identity. And your identity, first and foremost, is beloved. Cherished. Called. Whatever happens in the marketplace does not change what is true about who you are.*

There is one more piece of inner work I want to name, and it is the one most people resist the longest: getting support. Building a personal brand can be lonely, and the mental and emotional weight of putting yourself out there repeatedly, taking hits, navigating criticism, and doing it all over again is real. You were not designed to carry that alone. Find your people. Invest in coaching or community. Talk to someone who has been where you are going. The inner work does not happen in isolation. It happens in relationship.

The most resilient creators I know are not the ones with the thickest skin. They are the ones with the deepest roots, in their identity, in their community, in their faith. Thick skin is just armor. Deep roots are actual strength. Build your roots. The storms are coming for everyone. What matters is what you are anchored to when they arrive.

Rest Is Not the Enemy of Progress

I want to say something that might surprise you in a book about building: rest is not optional. It is not a reward you earn after you have done enough work. It is a requirement for the kind of work we are talking about here.

Creative work, the kind that is genuinely rooted in who you are, draws from a deep well. That well has to be filled. And it does not fill itself with more output. It fills with input, with rest, with experience, with silence, with the parts of life that have nothing to do with your brand. When you run your well dry chasing consistency, you stop creating from a full place and start creating from obligation. Your audience can feel the difference. You can feel the difference.

The creators who burn out are not the ones who worked too hard. They are the ones who stopped investing in the things that made the work worth doing. They poured out and never poured back in. They mistook exhaustion for discipline. Protect your creative energy the way you protect your brand reputation, because one directly feeds the other. A rested, full, genuinely inspired creator will always outperform a depleted one, no matter how many hours the depleted one puts in.

> *Even God rested on the seventh day. Not because He was tired, but because rest is built into the design of a sustainable life. If rest is woven into creation itself, it is not something to feel guilty about. It is something to honor.*

Praying Over What You Build

I want to say something that might feel unusual in a branding book: I pray over what I build. Before launches. Before big decisions. Before I say yes to something that feels right and before I say no to something that feels wrong. I bring my work into my faith life, not as a formality but because I genuinely believe that what I am building is not fully mine. It was assigned to me. And assignments require communication with the one who gave them.

I share that not to make you feel like you need to do exactly what I do, but to give you permission to integrate your faith into your building in whatever way feels true to you. You do not have to compartmentalize. You do not have to leave the most important relationship of your life outside the door when you sit down to work. God is not only interested in Sunday. He is interested in Monday through Sunday, in the content strategy and the contract negotiation and the creative block and the breakthrough.

When you build from that integrated place, something shifts in the quality of what you create. It stops being just work and starts being worship. Not every piece of content has to be explicitly spiritual. But everything you create can be done with the intention of honoring God with the gifts He gave you. That intention is felt. Your audience may not be able to name it, but they will feel something different about what you make when it comes from that place. Build from there.

The Freedom of Staying Authentic

A personal testimony

I want to share something personal with you. Not to sell you on anything. Not to point you toward something I have built. Just to tell you how my calling became something real, because I think it might help you recognize yours.

For as long as I can remember, I have had a specific kind of frustration when I watched talented, gifted, called people in the entertainment and creative space shrink themselves down to fit someone else's idea of what was marketable. I watched people with genuine voices trade them in for whatever was trending. I watched creators who had something real to say go silent because the industry told them it was not the right sound, the right look, the right moment.

And something in me just could not let it go.

---

*I did not start with a business plan. I
started with a burden. A deep sense that I
was supposed to do something about what I
kept seeing.*

When You Know Your Calling

I believe God gives each of us a specific kind of vision. Not a general desire to do good, but a pointed, particular thing we are called to address. Mine was this: the authentic voices of creators in the entertainment industry needed to be protected, not polished away. They needed someone who would call them higher instead of smaller. Someone who would say, what God put in you is the thing, not the trend.

That calling is what became Good Day Agency. Not a strategy. Not a market opportunity I identified. A response to something I felt deeply and could not shake.

I want to be honest: building it was not easy, and I did not have a blueprint. I had conviction. I had a track record from Jaclynn Belts and everything I had learned from showing up authentically in my own creative work. And I had a genuine belief that if I built something rooted in that conviction, it would serve people well.

That belief turned out to be right. But even if it had not, I would have had to build it. Because it was mine to build.

> *Psalm 139:14 says we are fearfully and wonderfully made. I believe that includes the specific things that frustrate you, move you, and will not leave you alone. Those are not random feelings. They are often the shape of your calling.*

This Is Not About My Story

I am not telling you this so you will admire what I built. I am telling you this because I want you to look at your own life and ask:

what is the thing I cannot stop seeing? What is the problem I keep wanting to solve? What is the gap I keep wishing someone would fill?

Because that thing, that specific frustration or passion or vision, that is probably closer to your calling than anything on a list of profitable niches.

Good Day Agency is my story. You have your own. Maybe it is not an agency. Maybe it is a brand, a platform, a product, a community, a creative project. Maybe it is something that does not even have a name yet. But if there is something you keep feeling pulled toward, something that feels like it belongs to you, I want you to take that seriously.

John 8:32 says the truth will set you free. I have found that to be as true in building as in anything else. When you stop building what you think you should and start building what you actually are, something opens up. The work gets lighter. The audience finds you. The impact grows. Because you are finally doing the thing you were made to do.

What Your Calling Might Be Asking of You

- What do you keep seeing that others seem to walk past?
- What problem do you feel personally responsible for solving?
- What would you build even if nobody paid you, because the need is just that clear to you?

- What has God been preparing you for through every experience, success, and failure you have had?

Those questions are not rhetorical. Sit with them. Because the answers are pointing somewhere.

And wherever they point, that is where your brand begins. That is where your real work is. That is where freedom lives.

Build from there.

I will tell you what I have learned from watching people answer those questions honestly: the calling is almost never as far away as it seems. It is usually hiding in plain sight, dressed up as a frustration you keep coming back to, or a question you keep asking that nobody else seems to be asking, or a type of person you cannot stop wanting to help. The calling tends to live right at the intersection of your deepest passion and someone else's deepest need.

When you find that intersection, and you will, do not overthink it. Do not wait for more credentials or more clarity or more permission. Just begin. Build the first version, which will not be the best version, and trust that the best version will reveal itself as you go. That is how every real thing gets built. Not from a perfect plan but from a genuine start.

I spent years building before I had the language for what I was doing. I was just following the pull, responding to the burden, showing up for the thing I kept feeling responsible for. And slowly, over time, the shape of it became clear. The agency was not something I planned. It was something I grew into by being faithful to the calling one step at a time. I share that because I do not want you to feel like you need to see the whole staircase before you take the first step. You do not. You just need to see the next one.

What Following Your Calling Actually Looks Like

I want to be honest about something: following your calling rarely looks like a clean, confident march forward. In my experience, it looks a lot more like repeated small decisions to keep going even when you are not sure where you are going.

It looks like saying yes to the thing that scares you a little, because the fear is attached to something that matters to you. It looks like doing the work even when no one is watching yet, because you believe the work has value regardless of the audience. It looks like saying no to things that pay well but cost you something you cannot afford to lose, your voice, your integrity, your sense of self.

And it looks like coming back. Coming back after the failed launch. Coming back after the season when you doubted everything. Coming back after you tried something that did not work and had to sit with the discomfort of starting over. The most consistent marker of someone living in their calling is not that they never struggle. It is that they keep coming back to the thing they know they are supposed to be doing. The calling is what you return to. Everything else is just noise.

Detail 7: Your Audience Is Your Community

Stop Collecting Followers. Start Building People.

There is a word that gets thrown around a lot in the branding and marketing world. That word is audience. And I want to gently challenge the way most people think about it.

An audience watches. An audience consumes. An audience shows up when the content is good and disappears when it is not. An audience is built around what you do. A community is built around who you are.

The difference between those two things is everything.

An audience follows your content. A community follows you. Build the kind of brand that makes people feel like they belong to something bigger than a content calendar.

Here is the practical reality of community building that nobody talks about enough: it is slow at first. Building real relationships, earning real trust, creating a space where people actually feel safe enough to show up, that does not happen overnight. It happens through months and years of consistent, genuine showing up. Through responding to the person nobody noticed. Through sharing the content that did not go viral but was the most honest thing you wrote. Through being the same person at a thousand followers that you are at a hundred thousand.

The brands that have the most powerful communities are rarely the biggest. They are the most consistent. The most honest. The most clearly themselves. Size is not the goal. Depth is. And depth is built one genuine exchange at a time.

What Makes Someone Feel Like They Belong

Community is not a strategy. It is an outcome. And it happens when people consistently feel three things in connection with your brand.

They feel seen. This means your content reflects their real experience. Not the polished, aspirational version of their life but the actual one. When your content names something true for someone, they do not just like it. They feel found.

They feel safe. This means you have created a space where realness is welcomed. Safety is built through consistency. Every time you show up honestly, you give your community permission to do the same.

They feel invested. This means they care about what happens to you and to each other. That level of investment is only possible when the relationship is real and reciprocal.

The early church in Acts 2 did not grow because of great marketing. It grew because people saw the way the believers loved each other and wanted to be part of it. Authentic community has always been one of the most powerful forces in the world. Build one and you will never need to chase an algorithm again.

How to Actually Build Community

- Respond to comments like they matter, because they do. Not with a generic emoji. With a real response that shows you actually read what someone wrote.

- Ask questions and actually want the answers. Make your audience part of the conversation.

- Highlight your community members. Share their wins. Celebrate their milestones.

- Create spaces for them to connect with each other, not just with you.

- Be honest about your own journey. Vulnerability from you creates permission for vulnerability from them.

Community Is Your Most Durable Brand Asset

Platforms change. Algorithms shift. Trends die. But a community that is genuinely bonded to your voice and your values will follow you wherever you go.

When you build community instead of just audience, you build portability. Your brand lives in the relationship, not in any single platform. And that is a kind of freedom that no algorithm can take from you.

> *Hebrews 10:24 says to consider how we may spur one another on toward love and good deeds. Your brand, when it is rooted in something real, can actually spur people on. It can be the thing that encourages someone to take the step they have been afraid of. That is not just a business outcome. That is a calling.*

I want to close this chapter by addressing something that comes up constantly: the pressure to grow your numbers. Community and size are not the same thing. I have seen creators with fifty thousand followers who have almost no community, and creators with two thousand followers who have built something so tight and loyal and alive that the engagement puts bigger accounts to shame. Stop chasing size. Chase depth. A community of a thousand people who genuinely trust you and buy from you and tell their friends about you is worth infinitely more than a hundred thousand passive scrollers who barely register your name.

Build the kind of community where people feel like they found their people. That is the goal. When someone lands in your space and thinks, oh, this is my kind of place, you have done something that no algorithm can replicate and no trend can take away.

How to Make People Feel Found

I want to get specific here because I think community building often gets talked about in abstract terms that do not translate into real behavior. Making people feel found is not about posting inspirational content. It is about specificity.

When your content is specific, when it names a particular feeling or experience or struggle with precision, it does something that broad content cannot do. It makes the person reading it feel like you wrote it for them. They do not feel like one of many. They feel like the one. That feeling is the foundation of community. It is not created by size. It is created by specificity and honesty.

So go specific. Name the exact thing. Describe the exact feeling. Call out the exact scenario your audience is living through. The more precise you are, the more people will feel you are speaking directly to them. Counterintuitively, the more specific your content, the wider your reach, because the right people find it and share it with everyone they know who is living the same experience.

When Your Community Carries You

There is a moment that happens in the life of every creator who has built something real: the moment when the community starts to carry the brand forward without you having to push it. Someone shares your content in a group chat. A community member answers a question in your comments before you can. A follower introduces you to someone new as if you are someone they genuinely care about.

That is not marketing. That is love. And it only happens when the relationship is real. When people feel genuinely seen and served by what you are building, they become advocates in a way that no paid promotion can replicate. They talk about you in rooms you are not in. They recommend you to people who are exactly who you needed to reach. They defend you when someone unfairly criticizes you. That level of loyalty is not bought. It is built, slowly, through the kind of consistent, genuine showing up we have been talking about throughout this book.

Protect that. Do not trade it for a shortcut. The community you have built is the most valuable thing your brand owns. Guard it like it is, because it is irreplaceable.

Detail 8: Collaboration Over Competition

Your So-Called Competition Might Be Your Greatest Ally

I also want to say something about the collaborations that do not go as planned. Because they will happen. You will partner with someone whose work you respected and discover mid-project that your working styles clash, or that their values are not as aligned as they appeared, or that the chemistry that seemed obvious in conversation does not translate to the work. That is normal. It is not a failure of judgment. It is the reality of creative collaboration.

What matters is how you handle it. With grace. With honesty. With respect for what the other person is building even if this particular thing did not work. The creative world is smaller than it looks. How you exit a collaboration that is not working says as much about your brand as how you enter one that is.
The personal branding world can feel like a zero-sum game. Like there is only so much attention to go around and if someone else in your space is winning, that somehow means you are losing.

I want to dismantle that idea completely.

It is rooted in scarcity, and scarcity is a lie. There is not a fixed amount of success available in any given niche. The internet has connected billions of people. The need for authentic voices, genuine expertise, and real human connection is not shrinking. It is expanding every single day.

Nobody else can be you. Nobody else has your specific combination of experience, perspective, personality, and calling. Which means nobody else is actually your competition.

---

*Competition says there is not enough room
for all of us. Collaboration says we make
the room bigger together.*

How to Collaborate Well

- Choose collaborators whose values align with yours, not just whose numbers impress you.
- Give generously before you ask for anything. Share someone else's work. Recommend them. Champion them publicly.
- Be honest about what you each bring to the table. A good collaboration is about two people creating something together that neither could have created alone.
- Celebrate other creators in your space without an agenda.

This Principle Shaped Everything I Built

When I was building my own creative work, I kept running into the same wall: isolation. And I watched other creators hit the same wall. One of the things I felt called to address when I started building a professional home for creators was this exact thing. Not because it was a smart business strategy, but because I believed deeply that people were not meant to build alone. That conviction shaped the culture I tried to create.

> *Ecclesiastes 4:9 says two are better than one, because they have a good return for their labor. You were not meant to build alone. Find your people and build together.*

A Word on Healthy Boundaries in Collaboration

Collaboration does not mean saying yes to everything and everyone. Before any collaboration, ask yourself: does this person's work reflect values I genuinely stand behind? Would I be proud to have my name next to theirs?

If the answer to any of those is no or even maybe, that is important information. A collaboration that compromises your integrity is not growth. It is a trade you will eventually regret.

And when a collaboration does go well, say so publicly. Celebrate it. The creator economy functions better when people are generous with credit and visibility. If someone helped you, if a collaboration opened a door, if a peer's work inspired something in yours, acknowledge it. That generosity compounds. It builds a reputation for being someone people want to work with, which ultimately brings more and better opportunities back to you than any strategic positioning ever could.

How to Reach Out Without Feeling Transactional

One of the things I hear most from creators is that they want to connect with peers they admire but they do not know how to do it without it feeling like a pitch. Here is what I have found: the cure for feeling transactional is leading with genuine.

Reach out to tell someone their work meant something to you. Not because you want something from them, just because it did. Reference something specific. Be human. Most people in the creator space are more accessible than they seem, and most of them are moved by a sincere message from someone who genuinely engaged with their work. That kind of outreach builds relationships in a way that a networking email never will.

You do not need a reason to reach out other than genuine appreciation and a real desire to connect. Start there. Let the relationship develop from that honest place. The collaborations that come from real relationships will always be more meaningful than the ones that come from strategy. And meaningful collaborations are the ones that actually move the needle, for your brand, for your audience, and for the other person too.

Rising Tides

There is a phrase I come back to often when I think about collaboration: rising tides lift all ships. When someone in your space wins, celebrate it genuinely. When someone creates something excellent, say so publicly. When you see a creator who is clearly doing the work with integrity, champion them even if they have nothing to offer you in return.

That kind of generosity does something that strategic positioning never can. It builds your reputation as someone who is for people, not just for themselves. And the creative world, which sometimes feels enormous, is actually quite small. The people you genuinely champion today will remember it. The doors you open for others without asking what is in it for you will often open back for you in ways you did not expect and could not have planned.

I have built some of my most meaningful professional relationships not through pitching or positioning but through simply being someone who showed up for others consistently and without an agenda. That is a long game, and it is one of the most reliable games I know.

I want to add something about rest that I think our culture has made us feel guilty about: you are allowed to step back. You are allowed to take a week, or two, or more when life demands it, and come back to your platform when you are genuinely ready. The creators who treat rest as a failure tend to burn out completely. The creators who build rest into their rhythm come back stronger, with more to say, with a clearer sense of why they are doing this.

Your audience will wait for you if what you are building is real. If the only thing keeping them is the frequency of your output, that is important information about the depth of connection you have built. But if you have done the work of genuine community building, a brief absence will not cost you what you have built. It might even deepen it, by reminding your audience that you are a real person with a real life, not a content machine.

Detail 9: Managing Your Digital Footprint

Show Up Everywhere Without Burning Out Anywhere

One of the most common questions I get from creators is some version of this: do I need to be on every platform?

The short answer is no. The long answer is also no, but with a lot more nuance attached to it.

You do not need to be everywhere. You need to be somewhere consistently, and you need to show up there as your full self. One platform done with depth and consistency will always outperform five platforms done halfheartedly and sporadically.

Your Home Base vs. Your Outposts

Think of your digital presence in two categories. Your home base is the one platform where you do your deepest work. Your outposts are everywhere else. They serve a specific purpose: discovery. Outpost content is lighter, more digestible, and designed to pull people toward your home base. These are doors. Your home base is the house.

The Art of Repurposing Without Watering Down

One piece of content can live in many different forms without you having to create from scratch every single time. A long-form blog post becomes a podcast episode becomes three Instagram carousels becomes a newsletter edition becomes a series of quotes. The core idea is the same. The format shifts to match the platform.

- Long-form content establishes depth and authority.
- Medium-form content maintains connection and delivers consistent value.
- Short-form content reaches new people and creates entry points into your world.

Protecting Your Brand Reputation Online

The internet has a memory, and it is not always kind. Post as the person you are becoming, not just the person you are today.

> *Proverbs 22:1 says a good name is more desirable than great riches. Your reputation is your most valuable brand asset. Protect it not by being perfect but by being consistently honest, consistently kind, and consistently willing to own your mistakes.*

Avoiding Burnout in a Content-Driven World

Content burnout is real and it is one of the leading reasons creators abandon their brands entirely. The antidote is building a content rhythm that is sustainable from the beginning.

- Batch create when you are in a flow state.
- Build a content bank for the weeks when life is heavy or creativity is low.

- Give yourself permission to be human on your platform. You do not owe your audience daily content. You owe them honesty.

- Protect your creative inputs. You cannot pour from an empty vessel. Life fills the well that content draws from.

A final word on digital footprint: do not underestimate the long game of searchability. The content you create today will be discoverable by people who have not met you yet, people who will find you six months or two years from now through a search, a share, or a recommendation. Every piece of content you put out is a door that stays open. This is why quality and consistency matter more than volume. You are not just creating for today's audience. You are building an archive that works for you while you sleep.

Think of your body of content like a library. Each piece you create is a book on the shelf. The more books you have, the more likely someone is to find the one that changes everything for them. Your job is not to go viral once. It is to keep adding books. Keep showing up. Keep contributing something real. The library grows over time, and so does its reach.

What You Do Not Have to Share

Authenticity does not mean transparency about everything. I want to be very clear about this because I think it is one of the most misunderstood ideas in the personal branding space. Being authentic does not mean giving the internet access to every part of your life. It means that what you do share is genuinely true.

You get to decide what is public and what is private. Your family, your relationships, your struggles that are still too fresh, your opinions on topics that are not yours to wade into publicly. None of that has to be on your platform. Authenticity lives inside the boundaries you choose, not outside them. The version of you that shows up in your content can be completely real and completely bounded at the same time.

What matters is that the boundaries are chosen intentionally rather than defensively. You are not hiding who you are. You are protecting what is sacred while sharing what serves your community. There is a meaningful difference between those two things. Build your content life in a way that you can sustain, that does not cost you your peace, and that still allows you to show up fully for the people who are listening. That is the standard.

I keep a note in my phone that I add to throughout the day. A thought that surfaced during a conversation. Something that frustrated me about the industry. A moment with someone that reminded me why I do this work. Most of those notes never become content. But some of them become the most resonant things I share, because they come from real life rather than from sitting down and trying to think of something to say.

The creators who never run out of things to say are not more creative than you. They are more attentive. They have trained themselves to notice the moments that matter and trust that those moments are worth sharing. That is a skill you can develop. Start noticing. Start writing things down. The content will follow.

Protecting Your Peace Online

Managing your digital footprint is not just about what you post. It is also about what you consume. The accounts you follow, the comment sections you linger in, the comparison spirals you allow yourself to scroll through at midnight, those things shape your creative output more than most people realize. If your digital diet is full of content that makes you feel behind, small, or inadequate, that feeling will find its way into how you show up for your own audience.

Be intentional about your inputs. Follow accounts that inspire you without triggering comparison. Unfollow without guilt anything that consistently makes you feel worse about your own work. Turn off notifications that fragment your focus during your most creative hours. Set boundaries around how much time you spend consuming versus creating. Your creative well does not fill from a scroll. It fills from silence, from real experience, from conversations that go somewhere, from the kind of rest that actually restores.

The most original content creators I know are almost never the ones glued to every trend and platform update. They are the ones who spend enough time away from the screen that they actually have something to say when they come back to it. Protect that space fiercely. The algorithm will always be there. Your creative edge is more fragile. Guard it accordingly.

Detail 10: Your Brand in Real Life

Personal Branding Happens Offline Too

We spend so much time talking about personal branding in the context of the internet that I think we sometimes forget something important: you are your brand everywhere. Not just on camera, not just on your profile, not just when you are creating content.

You are your brand in the meeting room. At the conference. In the hallway conversation. At the dinner table. In the way you treat the person who cannot do anything for you right now.

Your reputation is built in the spaces between the content. Who you are when no one is filming is the truest version of your brand.

Networking Without Losing Yourself

You can network as yourself. Walk into any room and simply be curious about the people in it. Ask real questions. Listen like you actually care about the answers. Follow up because you actually want to continue the conversation, not because you need something.

How You Show Up in Rooms Matters

- Be genuinely interested, not just interesting. People remember how you made them feel far more than what you said about yourself.

- Put the phone down. Presence is one of the rarest and most respected gifts you can give another person.

- Follow up on what you said you would do. Reliability is a brand statement.

- Be the same person in every room. Any gap between your online brand and your offline self will eventually surface.

Public Speaking as Brand Building

If you have the opportunity to speak publicly, take it. Speaking is one of the most powerful ways to establish your brand authority and deepen trust with the people who are already following you.

You do not need to be a polished professional speaker to start. You just need to be willing to share what you know, from a place of genuine care for the people in front of you. Start small. Say yes to opportunities before you feel ready. The stage grows as you grow.

> *Isaiah 50:4 speaks of having an instructed tongue, to know the word that sustains the weary. I believe every person who has been called to build a brand has been given something to say that will sustain someone. Your voice, live and in person, carries a power that goes beyond content strategy. Use it.*

Your Everyday Life Is Brand Research

Everything you experience feeds your brand. Pay attention to your life. Take notes. Ask questions. Stay curious. The richest content you will ever create will come not from sitting down to manufacture something but from noticing what is already happening inside you and around you.

I want to go back to something I said at the beginning of this chapter: you are your brand everywhere. That includes how you treat people who cannot do anything for you. The assistant at the event. The person at the check-in table. The new creator who has ten followers and is just starting out. How you show up for people who offer you nothing in return says everything about the kind of brand, and the kind of person, you actually are.

The digital world amplifies what already exists. If you are generous offline, that generosity will find its way into your content. If you are genuinely curious about people in real life, that curiosity will show up in how you engage with your community online. Your brand is not a performance you switch on. It is an overflow of who God made you to be. So invest in walking closely with that calling. The rest follows from there.

The Power of Being Fully Present

In a world that is constantly pulling for our attention, one of the most radical things you can do, both for your relationships and for your brand, is to be fully present in the room you are actually in. Not half-present while your mind is composing a caption about the experience. Actually, completely present.

This matters for your brand because presence is the prerequisite for connection, and connection is the foundation of everything we have talked about in this book. You cannot genuinely connect with someone while you are simultaneously documenting the connection for content. At some point you have to put the phone down and just be there. The memory of how you made someone feel will outlast any post you could have made about the moment.

Some of the most powerful brand-building moments I have ever had happened in conversations where nothing was recorded. A late-night conversation at a conference. A phone call that turned into a two-hour exchange about craft and calling. A moment where I told someone the truth they needed to hear and watched something open up in them. None of those were content. All of them were impact. And impact, whether or not it is documented, is the whole point.

Get in Rooms You Have to Grow Into

One of the most accelerating things you can do for your brand, and for yourself, is intentionally put yourself in rooms where you are not yet the most accomplished person in the space. The rooms that stretch you. The conferences where you have to introduce yourself to people who are further along. The tables where you have to listen more than you talk.

There is a version of personal branding that is entirely self-referential. You only talk to the people who already follow you, consume content from the people who validate what you already believe, and stay in communities where you are always the expert. That version feels safe. But it stops your growth quietly, over time, until one day you realize that your perspective has not expanded in years.

The most interesting creators I know are the ones who are perpetually students. Not because they lack confidence in what they know, but because they are genuinely curious about what they do not know yet. That curiosity is alive in their content. It keeps their voice fresh. It keeps their audience engaged. Because watching someone grow in real time is one of the most compelling things a brand can offer.

So say yes to the room that intimidates you a little. Introduce yourself to the person whose work you admire but feel unqualified to approach. Sit at the table and contribute. You belong there not because you have arrived but because you are in the process of becoming. That process, done out loud and honestly, is one of the most powerful things your brand can be.

Detail 11: Knowing When to Say No

Protecting Your Brand When the Money Is on the Table

I want to talk about one of the hardest things you will face as your brand grows. It is not the fear of failure. It is not the critics. It is not the algorithm changes or the platform shifts or the creative blocks.

It is the moment when an opportunity arrives that does not fully align with who you are, and it comes with a check attached.

That moment is a test. And how you handle it will say more about your brand than almost anything you will ever post.

What That Moment Actually Feels Like

Let me describe the scenario because I think naming it specifically helps. The email comes in. Or the DM. Or the call. And whatever is being offered sounds good. More than good, honestly. The money is real. The name attached to it is recognizable. The opportunity has a kind of shine to it that makes it easy to talk yourself into.

And then there is this little thing. Barely a whisper. Something in your gut that goes hmm. Maybe the product does not totally reflect what you actually believe in. Maybe the brand has values that are adjacent to yours but not quite yours. Maybe the positioning they want you to take feels a little off from how you actually talk. It is not a screaming red flag. It is more like a yellow flag. And yellow flags are the dangerous ones because they are so easy to explain away.

So you start negotiating with yourself. You come up with reasons why it is fine. You think about what the money would do. You remind yourself that it is just one post, one campaign, one collaboration. You tell yourself you are being too precious about your brand and that real business people take real opportunities. And somewhere in the middle of all that internal negotiation, you know. You already know. You just have not said it out loud yet.

I have said yes when I knew the answer was no. I am not going to sit here and pretend I have always gotten this right. I have taken opportunities that looked great on paper and felt wrong in my body from the minute I agreed to them. And every single time, the cost was higher than the check. Not always financially. Sometimes in energy. Sometimes in the quiet erosion of something I could not fully name until it was already gone. The thing about integrity is you do not notice how much you have until you start spending it. And once it is spent, the rebuilding takes much longer than the spending did.

So now I have a rule. When the little hmm shows up, I do not negotiate with it. I investigate it. I sit with it long enough to understand what it is trying to tell me. And if I cannot get fully comfortable, not just financially comfortable but values comfortable, the answer is no. Every time. No matter how shiny the opportunity is.

Every yes you give to something that does not fit is a no to something that does. Your time, your platform, and your audience's trust are not unlimited resources. Spend them wisely.

How to Evaluate an Opportunity for Brand Alignment

- Does this product, brand, or person genuinely reflect something I believe in?
- Would my most loyal community members feel proud of this, or would they feel confused or disappointed?
- Ten years from now, will I be proud that I put my name on this?
- Am I saying yes because this is right, or because I am afraid of saying no?
- Does this move me toward the brand I am building or away from it?

Matthew 6:24 says you cannot serve two masters. When you try to serve both your authentic calling and the opportunity that compromises it, you end up serving neither well. Clarity of purpose requires clarity of commitment.

How to Say No Gracefully

- Be prompt. Once you know it is not right, communicate that clearly and quickly.

- Be honest but kind. A simple acknowledgment that the fit is not right is sufficient.

- Leave the door open when it is genuine. Relationships are long.

- Do not apologize excessively. A clean, confident no is more respectful than an overqualified, apologetic one.

The Long Game of Integrity

Every time you say no to the wrong thing, you are saying yes to the right thing. You are protecting the trust of your audience. You are preserving your credibility.

Creators who are willing to say no to misaligned opportunities tend to attract better aligned ones. Integrity has a magnetic quality. When the market knows that you cannot be bought cheaply, your value goes up.

That is the long game. And the long game is the only game worth playing.

Here is something practical: build your values list before opportunities arrive. Write out the three to five things that are non-negotiable for your brand, the products you will never promote, the messaging you refuse to attach your name to. Keep it somewhere you can find it when the pressure is on. Written values are a contract with yourself. It is much harder to talk yourself out of something when you already made the decision.

The no is not the end of the conversation. It is the beginning of clarity. Every boundary you set, every misaligned deal you walk away from, every opportunity you turn down because it does not fit who you are, those decisions compound over time into something powerful. A reputation. A standard. A brand that people trust because they have watched you choose integrity over and over again, even when it cost you something.

Matthew 6:33 says seek first the kingdom and all these things will be added to you. I have watched that be true in business. When you keep the main thing the main thing, when you protect your calling instead of chasing every check, the right things tend to find their way to you. Not always fast. But faithfully.

Detail 12: Legacy Over Likes

Building Something That Outlasts the Algorithm

Legacy is built in the ordinary moments. In the caption you wrote at midnight that came from somewhere real. In the message you sent to the follower who was struggling. In the decision to stay true to your values when the shortcut was right in front of you and the check was good. Nobody is watching most of these moments. Nobody will ever write about them. But they are the actual architecture of a lasting brand.

I want you to start thinking about your brand as something you are building not just for today's audience but for the person who will find it five years from now at exactly the right moment. That piece of content you are debating whether to post, the one that feels too vulnerable or too specific or too small, that might be exactly what someone needs to hear the day they find it. Build with that person in mind. Build like it matters, because it does.

I want to ask you a question that I think about often, one that has shaped every major decision I have made in my own brand and in everything I have built.

What do you want people to say about what you built, ten years from now?

Not what metrics you hit. Not what your follower count peaked at. Not what your best launch number was. What do you want the story to be? What do you want to have meant?

Likes are a measurement of a moment. Legacy is a measurement of a life. You were not called to optimize for moments. You were called to build something that endures.

The Danger of Metric-Driven Building

Metrics are useful. I am not telling you to ignore your analytics or pretend that numbers do not matter in a business context. They do. But metrics are a tool for understanding your brand, not the purpose of it.

When metrics become the purpose, something shifts. You start making decisions based on what will perform rather than what is true. I have watched talented creators start out building something genuinely meaningful and slowly trade the meaning for the metrics. And one day they looked at what they had built and did not recognize it anymore. The numbers were fine. The soul was gone.

Do not let that happen to you.

What Legacy Actually Looks Like

Legacy is not about being famous. It is about being faithful. Faithful to your calling. Faithful to your audience. Faithful to the values that made your brand worth following in the first place.

Legacy looks like the person who found your content at their lowest point and pulled themselves out of it. The creator you mentored who went on to build something beautiful. The community you built that kept meeting long after you stepped back from it.

Proverbs 13:22 says a good person leaves an inheritance for their children's children. What you build with your brand can outlast you. The content you create today could find someone ten years from now who needed exactly that word in exactly that season. Build with that kind of intentionality.

Shifting From Short-Term Thinking to Long-Term Vision

- Create content that will still be valuable a year from now. Evergreen content rooted in timeless principles compounds in value over time.

- Invest in relationships more than reach. The person you pour into genuinely today may be the one who carries your message further than any algorithm ever could.

- Document your journey honestly. Your journey is someone else's map.

- Build systems and structures that can grow beyond you. A business that only works when you are personally operating every part of it is not a legacy. It is a job.

- Mentor someone. Share what you know. Open doors for people coming behind you.

The Multiplying Effect of Mentorship

I want to spend a moment on that last point because I think it is one of the most underrated things a creator or brand builder can do, and it is almost never talked about in the context of brand growth.

When you invest in someone coming behind you, something happens that goes beyond generosity. You clarify your own thinking. The act of putting what you know into words for someone else forces you to understand it at a deeper level. You see your own journey from a new angle. You remember how far you have come. And you build a relationship with someone who, if you are genuinely invested in their growth, will become one of your most loyal advocates.

Legacy is not built by hoarding what you know. It is built by giving it away. Every person you pour into genuinely carries a piece of your impact forward. They carry it into rooms you will never enter, to audiences you will never reach, in ways you cannot predict or plan. That is legacy working through people. It is the most powerful and the most human form of impact available to you.

So find someone to pour into. It does not have to be a formal mentorship. It can be a DM answering a question you once had. A voice note to a creator you believe in. An introduction made freely. A door held open. Start small. Start now. The ripple effect of genuine investment in another person is one of the most beautiful things you will ever witness.

2 Timothy 4:7 says I have fought the good fight, I have finished the race, I have kept the faith. That is my prayer for every person reading this book. Not that you will go viral. Not that you will hit every revenue goal. But that you will finish. That you will stay true. That you will keep the faith in what you were called to build, all the way to the end.

Build the kind of brand that still matters when the metrics are gone. Build something true. Build something that serves. Build something that lasts.

Legacy does not happen by accident, and it is not reserved for people who become household names. Legacy is simply the accumulated impact of showing up faithfully, for a long time, in service of something that genuinely matters. It is the creator who kept teaching long after the views dropped. The entrepreneur who kept serving their community long after the trend moved on. The builder who kept building even when nobody was watching.

You do not need a large platform to leave a legacy. You need a faithful one. Show up with integrity for the people who are actually in your corner, serve them well, and let the impact compound over time. Legacy is not about how many people you reach. It is about how deeply you reach the people you do. Go deep. Stay faithful. The rest takes care of itself.

What You Leave in People

I want to close this chapter with something that I think gets overlooked in almost every conversation about building a brand: the most enduring part of your legacy will not be the content you created. It will be the way you made people feel about themselves.

The creator who made someone believe they could start the thing they had been afraid to start. The entrepreneur whose honesty about their own journey gave someone else permission to be honest about theirs. The brand that held the door open just long enough for someone who needed to walk through it. That is legacy. That is the kind of impact that does not show up in analytics but lives in people for years.

So as you think about what you are building and why, ask yourself this alongside all the strategic questions: who am I becoming in the process of building this? Because your brand is a byproduct of your character. The more you invest in becoming a person of genuine integrity, generosity, and faith, the more that investment will show up in everything you create. You cannot separate the builder from the thing being built. They are the same.

Build something worthy of the gifts God gave you. Build something that serves the people He meant for you to reach. Build something you will be proud of when the metrics no longer matter. That is the whole assignment. Everything else is just detail.

Conclusion: Start Now, Not Later

Okay. We made it.

We went through twelve Details, a case study, a bonus chapter, a testimony, and more honesty than most branding books are willing to put on paper. And if you have read all the way to this page, I want you to know something: that says a lot about you. Most people skim. Most people read the first chapter and the last page and call it done. You did not do that. You stayed. That tells me you are serious about this. And serious is exactly what it takes.

What I Actually Want For You

I want to tell you what I genuinely want for you as you close this book, because I think it matters that you hear it.

I do not want you to go viral. I mean, if that happens, great, congratulations, enjoy it while it lasts, it will pass. But that is not the thing I am hoping for you.

I want you to build something that feels like yours. Something that when you sit down to create it, you feel that particular kind of tired that only comes from doing something that actually matters to you. I want you to have an audience that feels like community. I want you to make money from work that aligns with who you are so completely that charging for it never feels like selling out.

I want you to have the experience I had with Jaclynn Belts, where I built something for the love of it and it turned into something real. Not because I was the most talented person in the room. Not because I had the best strategy. Because I was the most authentically myself person in the room. And that, it turns out, is the competitive advantage nobody talks about enough.

I want you to have that. All of it.

A Few Things I Need You to Remember

Before you close this book and go build something, let me leave you with the things I come back to when I need a reminder myself.

Your brand is not your identity. It is an expression of your identity. When it is not performing the way you hoped, that is not a verdict on your worth. It is data. Use it.

The slow seasons are not wasted. They are where the foundation gets laid. Every creator who built something lasting went through a stretch where nothing seemed to be working. You do not hear about those stretches because they do not make for a good headline. But they are real and they are necessary and you are going to be okay.

Being yourself is the work. Not the easy part of the work. The actual work. The discipline of not drifting, not performing, not slowly becoming a more palatable version of yourself for the sake of the numbers, that is what this whole book has been about. Do not skip that part.

And finally: you have been called. Not in a vague inspirational sense. In a specific, practical, God-ordained sense. The gifts you carry, the perspective you have, the experiences that shaped you, those are not random. They are intentional. You were made for something on purpose. The brand you build is simply the vehicle for getting that something out into the world where it belongs.

If you have a passion and you are
authentic, you can build a brand that is SO
YOU. And that brand can absolutely,
undeniably change your life.

Ephesians 2:10 says we are God's handiwork, created in Christ Jesus to do good works, which He prepared in advance for us to do. Your work matters. Your voice matters. The platform you build, no matter the size, is part of something bigger than you can fully see from here.

One Last Thing

I want you to know that I wrote this book because I believe in you. Not in a generic, everybody-gets-a-trophy kind of way. I mean I genuinely believe that the specific person reading this sentence, with your specific story and your specific gifts and your specific calling, has something to offer the world that nobody else can offer. I have spent my career in rooms with talented people. And the ones who change things are never the most impressive ones. They are the most honest ones.

Be honest. Be consistent. Build from who you actually are instead of who you think the market wants you to be. Say no to the things that compromise you. Say yes to the things that light you up. Rest when you need to. Come back when you are ready. And on the days when all of it feels like too much, come back to this book. Come back to the reason you started. Come back to the version of yourself who picked this up in the first place. That person knew something. I promise you, they knew something.

Now go build the thing. The world has been waiting for it.

The world is waiting for the real, passionate, one-of-a-kind you.

Now go build it.

Jaclynn Buchanan